Mysterious Encounters

ANGELS

BY RACHEL LYNETTE

KIDHAVEN PRESS

An imprint of Thomson Gale, a part of The Thomson Corporation

THOMSON

——✶——™

GALE

Detroit • New York • San Francisco • San Diego • New Haven, Conn. • Waterville, Maine • London • Munich

© 2007 Thomson Gale, a part of The Thomson Corporation.

Thomson and Star Logo are trademarks and Gale and KidHaven Press are registered trademarks used herein under license.

For more information, contact
KidHaven Press
27500 Drake Rd.
Farmington Hills, MI 48331-3535
Or you can visit our Internet site at http://www.gale.com

Picture Credits:
Cover photo: Stephen Goldblatt/HBO/The Kobal Collection; © Alinari Archives/CORBIS, 41; © Archivo Iconografico, S.A./CORBIS, 8; Jose Azel/Aurora/Getty Images, 35; © Brooklyn Museum of Art/CORBIS, 24; © Christie's Images/CORBIS, 6; © David Crossland/Alamy, 17; © Araldo de Luca/CORBIS, 5; © Denny Ellis/Alamy, 26; © Gerrit Greve/CORBIS, 29; © Apollo Icdag/zefa/CORBIS, 21; © Images.com/CORBIS, 33; Imagno/Hulton Archive/Getty Images, 11; © Mark A. Johnson/CORBIS, 37; Mary Evans Picture Library, 15, 38; Scala/Art Resource, NY, 18; Time & Life Pictures/Getty Images, 30

LIBRARY OF CONGRESS CATALOGING-IN-PUBLICATION DATA

Lynette, Rachel.
    Angels / by Rachel Lynette.
        p. cm. — (Mysterious encounters)
    Includes bibliographical references (p.) and index.
    Contents: Angels all around—Angels that bring comfort—Angels with a message—Saved by an angel.
        ISBN 0-7377-3607-0 (hard cover : alk. paper) 1. Angels—Juvenile literature.
    I. Title. II. Series.
        BL477.L96 2006
        202'.15—dc22
                                                                    2006009617

Printed in the United States of America

Contents

Chapter 1

Angels All Around

According to a May 2004 Gallup poll, 78 percent of Americans believe in angels. Many of these people believe that angels are all around. They believe angels see everything and help people when they need it. Many people also think they have their own **guardian angel**. A guardian angel is one that has been assigned to watch over a specific person and keep him or her safe. Some people even say that they can communicate with their guardian angels.

What Is an Angel?

Many people who have encountered angels report that the angel communicated with them in some way.

A sixteenth-century painting shows a protective angel. Some people believe that their own guardian angel watches over them.

A white-robed angel appears before three women at Jesus's tomb.

Indeed, the word *angel* means "messenger." Some people believe that angels are messengers from God. Western religions—Christianity, Judaism, and Islam—all have many mentions of angels in their spiritual texts. These scriptures say that God created angels to serve him.

Angels have often been portrayed in books and movies as people who have died and gone to heaven. While Western religions support the idea that people who have died may go to heaven and dwell among the angels, most do not teach that people actually become angels. Rather, angels are a completely different kind of being. They are spiritual beings without form, although they may take the shape of humans or even animals. They do not grow old, and they live forever.

Even though angels are thought to be formless, angel images appear frequently in Western culture. These images appear not just in religious art but also in books and greeting cards and on jewelry. Usually these angels are depicted as a human with large white wings, dressed in a flowing white robe. Often these figures have a **halo**, which appears as a ring of light encircling the head. They are also shown as chubby, naked babies with wings. However, not everyone who has reported an encounter with an angel saw a winged adult, and very few saw a winged baby. Many times a person who has an encounter does not even see an angel, but rather feels it as a presence. This makes sense since angels are not believed to have physical bodies.

Dark Angels

Most angel encounters are positive and uplifting experiences. But some people have had negative or frightening encounters with angels. These people believe they came in contact with dark angels, sometimes called fallen angels, devils, or demons.

According to the Bible, these dark angels rebelled against God. They were led by an angel named Lucifer or Satan. There was a big battle between the dark angels and those that remained faithful to God. When the dark angels lost, they were cast out of heaven and sent to the fiery pits of hell.

Like other angels, dark angels are also believed to be spiritual beings with no form who can take any

In this painting from an altarpiece, good angels battle monstrous dark angels who rebelled against God.

shape they wish. Many people who have had encounters with dark angels report seeing horrible, monstrous creatures with scaly skin, reptilian eyes, claws, and tails. Others report seeing a devil much like those shown in books and movies—with red clothing and skin, horns, and a tail. However, some people say that the demon they saw looked like a kind angel. Dark angels are believed to be masters of **deception**, so these people may have seen a dark angel in disguise.

People who have encountered dark angels say that the demon usually wanted something from them. A dark angel may want someone to act in a bad way or may try to tempt someone into trading away his or her soul. There are also many stories of **demonic possession**. This happens when a demon takes over a person's body and uses it for its own purposes.

What Are Angel Encounters Like?

Encounters with angels take many forms. They almost always involve just one person, though there have been accounts of angels visiting several people at once. Angels communicate with humans in different ways. People have reported seeing, hearing, feeling, and even smelling angels!

Sometimes a person who has encountered an angel reports seeing the traditional angel image complete with wings and halo. But more often, the angel looks like an ordinary person. The person is sometimes very beautiful or handsome and is wearing white, but usually, it is a person who would blend into any crowd. In many accounts, the angel appears from nowhere and disappears mysteriously.

Sometimes angels are seen not in human form, but rather as light. Many people have reported seeing a circle or beam of light that could not be explained by the Sun, lamps, or any other light source. This kind of angel encounter often occurs when someone dies.

People who believe they have heard angels often report hearing bells or beautiful music that seems to have no earthly source. They think these sounds are angels singing. Some people have said they heard a voice in their head that was not their own. Other angel encounters have involved people hearing a voice when they were alone or hearing a voice that no one else could hear.

Sometimes people neither see nor hear an angel. Instead, the angel is felt or sensed. People have reported the feeling of being touched, even when no one else was around. Often this touch is a gentle stroke on the cheek or a pat on the back. Other people have said they felt as if a giant pair of wings were wrapped around them. The wings comforted them or made them feel safe. Sometimes the angel is not even felt as a physical presence. Some people

As in this painting of Saint Joseph and an angel, some people report sensing an angel's touch, rather than seeing it.

have described their angel encounters as feeling a divine presence or suddenly having an overwhelming feeling of peace or of being cared for.

Other people believe they have detected the presence of angels using their sense of smell. Many people have reported noticing a scent that could not be explained by anything in the area. The smell is always of something pleasant, like flowers.

Who Encounters Angels?

People from all walks of life all over the world have reported encountering angels. However, most angel encounters happen to people who are very religious or who have a strong belief in angels. Some people even do things to attract angels, such as saying special prayers. Children also seem to have more angel encounters than adults. Many people believe that children are by nature closer to the unseen world and more open to it.

Imaginary Angels

Children tend to have powerful imaginations. Some people believe that children who report seeing angels are really just imagining them, as they might imagine a scary monster or an invisible friend.

Often, an angel encounter happens at a critical time in a person's life. Some of the most dramatic angel encounters seem to occur in life-threatening situations. Many people have been saved from a violent death or healed from a fatal illness in ways that they believe could not have happened without the help of an angel.

Sometimes angels bring important messages. People have reported an angel giving them information that helps them to feel at peace in a difficult situation. Others have been told about something that will happen in the future. Some people have reported that the angel came with a command from God.

Angels also come to bring comfort. Many people who are dying report seeing angels in their last few days or moments of life. The angel is there as a calming presence and helps the person cross over from life to death. Angels may also offer understanding and reassurance to those who are grieving and to people who are very troubled or sad.

Sometimes people encounter an angel in answer to prayer, but sometimes the encounter is unexpected. In either case, the person almost always benefits in some way. Most people who encounter angels are grateful for the experience.

Chapter 2

Angels That Bring Comfort

Many people who encounter angels report feeling an overwhelming sense of peace or a feeling of being cared for and loved. Usually the person knows that the feeling is coming from an angel, even if he or she does not actually see one. If the angel can be seen, either as light, as an angelic image, or in human form, it may offer encouraging words or a gentle touch. The resulting feeling of peace can last for a few minutes, a few days, or even a lifetime. Even if the feeling passes, people who have been consoled by angels never forget the encounter and often draw comfort from the memory.

Wrapped in Wings

Gwenn Scott is an example of someone who was re-assured by an angel. Discouraged and sad, Scott was lying in bed in her dark room one night. Suddenly she saw a very bright, pea-sized light through her

In this illustration, an angel enfolds two wretched men in its wings to comfort them.

closed eyes. She heard a voice telling her to keep her eyes closed or she could be blinded. Scott obeyed, but the light was so bright that it still hurt her eyes. The light became an angel that she could see even through her closed eyelids.

The angel wrapped its wings around Scott until she was completely enfolded in them. She said later she felt "absolute love, peace and protection."[1] The angel told her that she was being watched over. The experience gave Scott a lasting sense of calm.

Comfort from Grief

Jennifer Helvey-Davis also received lasting peace from an angel encounter. She was twenty-one years old and living with her grandparents when she discovered that her beloved grandmother had died during the night. Helvey-Davis was overwhelmed with grief.

Helvey-Davis visited her grandmother's grave soon afterward. As she looked up at a cloudy sky, she suddenly saw what appeared to be a kind of gray starburst in front of the clouds. From the center of the starburst, an angelic being appeared. According to Helvey-Davis, "The being had long hair and a distinct heavy robe with a cord around the waist. The hands were stretched on the being's side with the palms facing upward. I couldn't see a face, yet these majestic wings opened broadly from behind the back of the image I saw."[2] Helvey-Davis estimates that, had the angel been on the ground, it would have been about 7 feet (2.1m) tall.

Helvey-Davis was amazed and fell to her knees with tears in her eyes. The angel nodded toward her and snapped its giant wings closed with a loud whooshing sound. Helvey-Davis looked away, and when she looked back toward the sky, the angel was gone.

A stone angel watches over a cemetery. Some people believe their departed loved ones live with the angels.

When Helvey-Davis returned to her car, she sketched a quick picture of the angel. She knew then that her grandmother was living with the angels. When she left the cemetery, she says, she felt "a strange feeling of peace and calm."[3]

The soft sounds of angel music are said to be soothing and peaceful.

Bedside Companion

Like Helvey-Davis, many people report being visited by angels in a cemetery. Another common place for angel encounters is a hospital. Both patients and their family members, as well as doctors and nurses, have reported seeing angels. One such patient was Sandy Smith, who was admitted to Grady Memorial Hospital in Delaware, Ohio, after a car accident. Smith had recently graduated from high school and was driving to a state park with a girlfriend for a camping trip. On the way, the car swerved and then rolled over several times.

When Smith woke up in the hospital after the accident, she was not seriously hurt, but she was alone and frightened. She desperately wanted her mother, but her mother had died six months earlier. She lost consciousness, and when she awoke again she found someone sitting next to her, holding her hand. The woman was dressed all in white. She had very pale skin and long, almost white hair.

The figure also produced a strange yet soothing noise, which Smith describes as "a fanlike whirring but deeper, like the beating of thousands of birds' wings."[4] It seemed as if a feeling of love was coming from the mysterious sound and filling the whole room. This calmed Smith, and she fell into a deep sleep.

When she awoke, a nurse was washing her face. Assuming the nurse was the same person who had been there earlier, Smith asked her to hold her hand and sing again. But the nurse said that the hospital was shorthanded that weekend and that she had not had time to sit with Smith. The nurse was also sure that no one else had been in Smith's room.

Smith has occasionally heard that same reassuring noise again. On the morning of her wedding day, the sound filled her room. Whenever she hears that special song, Smith feels that her angel is nearby.

Angelic Spirits

Sometimes people who are dying encounter angels who take away their fear and pain. Caregivers have often reported that in the last days or hours before death, the dying person seems to see and communicate with angelic spirits in the room. Some caregivers have even seen a glowing light or angelic figure ministering to the dying person. Melissa Deal Forth, for example, believes an angel visited her husband, Chris, in the hospital before he died of cancer.

Two days before Chris died, Melissa found him in the hospital chapel. He was talking with a man

Angels at Death

Some scientists think that during a person's last minutes of life, the brain manufactures comforting images, such as angels, to make dying easier and more peaceful.

Stone statues of angels are found in many places, a sign of strong belief in their existence.

Melissa had never seen before. Melissa was amazed because Chris was very sick and should not even have been able to get out of bed, much less walk down the hall.

The stranger with Chris was dressed in what looked like new work clothes: jeans, a flannel shirt, and work boots. Melissa could not tell how old he was. "There was no real age to him," she says. "No wrinkles. Just this perfectly smooth and pale, white, white skin and ice blue eyes. I've never seen that color blue on any human before. They were more the blue like some of those Husky dogs have. I'll never forget the eyes."[5]

Melissa left the two alone, and when Chris returned to his room he was smiling. He told her that the man had been his guardian angel. The angel reassured Chris that there was nothing to fear and left him with a feeling of peace. Chris died quietly two days later. Melissa says that she thinks about that angel every day. "I know what I saw, and I know it changes lives," she says. "Never, never will anyone be able to convince me that angels don't exist."[6] Like Melissa, most people who have been comforted by an angel are sure that they are real. To them, knowing that angels exist has a lasting, positive effect on their lives.

Chapter 3

Angels with a Message

Sometimes people encounter an angel with a message. Often the message consists of advice. The advice might be spiritual in nature. The person may be told not to lose faith in God or to follow a certain spiritual path. The advice could also be practical. People have reported having angels tell them which route to take to avoid getting lost or where a misplaced item is located. The message could also be a piece of important information that the person does not yet know. Many people have had encounters in which an angel tells them that someone close to them has died.

An artist depicts a man's journey to heaven, escorted by angels, soon after his death.

An Angel for Helen

An angel told a little girl named Helen about her grandmother's death before her parents did. Her grandmother lived with Helen's family and had been sick for a long time. When she died, Helen's parents decided it would be better not to tell their daughter until the body had been taken away. Helen was taken out for the morning. After she returned home, she ran upstairs to see her grandmother. She was puzzled to find the bed empty. When she turned to go back downstairs, a man dressed all in white, with white hair, was standing near the door. Helen asked who he was, and the man replied, "I am an angel. I have come to take your grandmother to Heaven."[7] A few minutes later, Helen's mother started to tell her about her grandmother's death, but Helen interrupted her. She told her mother that the angel had said her grandmother was in heaven.

Dale's Angel

Sometimes an angel comes not to tell of a death, but rather to reassure someone that a loved one will be

Forgotten Knowledge

People who encounter angels that tell them that someone has died might not have actually gotten the information from an angel. It could be that the person got the information from another source, such as overhearing a conversation, and then later forgetting where they had heard it.

okay. Dale was six years old when his father, a pilot, was suddenly called by the U.S. Air Force Reserve to fly to France. As the weeks passed, Dale became convinced that his father had been killed. He became very sad, **mourning** the loss of his father. No one could convince Dale that his father was still alive.

Then one night Dale saw a bright light in the corner of his room. The light grew into a female angel

A sculpture shows an angelic-looking man with a young boy and captures the sense of comfort that many find in angels.

who came to Dale's bed and held his hand. The angel assured Dale that his dad was fine and would be coming home soon. The angel told him, "I am watching over your father, Dale. I'll make sure he comes home safely to you when his job is finished."[8] Dale's spirits rose immediately. Both his mother and teacher were amazed at how quickly his mood improved. Dale remained peaceful and happy, and his father came back a few weeks later, safe and sound.

Miriam's Angel

Miriam was also reassured by an angel. Miriam was nineteen when her sister, Liz, was involved in a serious car accident. Her mother called her at work to tell her the devastating news, saying that Liz was in surgery and was not expected to survive. Miriam ran outside and hailed the nearest taxi. When she climbed in, she was surprised to find that another woman was already inside the cab.

The woman smiled kindly and told Miriam that she was also going to the hospital, so they could share the taxi. On the way, Miriam told the woman about the accident. When they got to the hospital, the two women walked up the driveway together. At the door, the woman told Miriam, "You must not worry. I know your sister will not die and all will be well."[9] Then she gave Miriam a gentle push toward the door. When Miriam turned back to hold the door open for the woman, she was astonished to find her gone and the driveway empty.

Miriam hurried into the waiting room. A sense of calm came over her and she reassured her sobbing mother that her sister would be okay. Liz survived the surgery and made a quick recovery. Thinking back on the experience later, Miriam was convinced that the kind woman was an angel.

Angel Warnings

Miriam's angel appeared in broad daylight and seemed like a real person, but sometimes people encounter angels when they are asleep. Marilynn Carlson Webber's angels came to her in a dream. In it, she saw four angels who were dressed all in black and appeared to be in mourning. She asked them why they were so sad, and one of them replied, "Because you are dying. If something is not done soon, you will die."[10]

Webber woke from her dream and told her husband about it. He took her to the doctor the next morning, and the doctor ran some tests. One showed a cancerous **tumor** that had to be removed right away. Webber had the surgery and made a full recovery. The doctor told her that if she had waited, the cancer would have spread and Webber probably would have died. Webber believes that her angelic message of warning saved her life.

Charles Lindbergh's Angels

The famous pilot Charles Lindbergh also reported being helped by angels. In May 1927 Lindbergh became the first person to fly alone across the Atlantic

An artist depicts a grieving angel. Some say that angels mourn sad events.

Ocean. He made the historic trip in his plane, the *Spirit of St. Louis.*

The journey took 33.5 hours. Lindbergh had to stay awake the entire time. For several hours his plane traveled through a thick fog. Twenty-three hours into his flight, Lindbergh encountered what he describes as "friendly, vaporlike shapes, without substance, able to vanish or appear at will."[11] These forms had a human shape and could pass through the walls of his plane as if they were not there. Some of these beings stayed in the plane with Lindbergh, floating just behind his shoulders. The forms spoke to him, giving him advice

Famed pilot Charles Lindbergh believed that angels advised him during his historic transatlantic flight.

on the flight, discussing navigation problems and re-assuring him. In addition to giving him information, these mysterious angels helped to keep Lindbergh awake.

People like Lindbergh who have received messages from angels usually appreciate the message, even if it is a sad one. When a person follows the advice of an angel, it can have profound effects on his or her life. People have reported moving, changing jobs, and even marrying because an angel told them to do so.

Chapter 4

Saved by an Angel

There are many stories of angels saving people from accidental death. A great number of these encounters happen on the road. Angels keep people from being run over, prevent accidents, and protect people from serious injury if their car does crash. Angels also save people from poisonous snakes and fires, and rescue people who are drowning or lost in snowstorms. This angelic help can come in many ways. Often, aid comes in the form of a person who does or says something to prevent an accident and then disappears mysteriously. Sometimes people hear a voice giving them instructions that save their lives. Other people have felt hands lifting them out of harm's way or have seen an angelic figure appear just in time to save them.

Angel on the Road

Ten-year-old Linda Harmitz did not actually see the angel that saved her life, but she did see its hands. Linda was riding in a car with her grandfather when he began to moan. Just as he accelerated into a busy

A modern artist captures the powerful touch of an angel's hands.

intersection, Linda's grandfather clutched at his heart and fell over, almost on top of her. Linda managed to get out from under her grandfather and grab the steering wheel. Her grandfather's foot was jammed against the gas pedal, and the car was moving quickly.

Linda was terrified, sure that the car would crash. She prayed, "Please God, oh please, help me get through this traffic and park the car and if you're too busy just now, please send an angel to help me."[12] As soon as Linda said the prayer, she felt a touch on her shoulder and saw two hands on the steering wheel. The angelic hands steered the car through traffic and into an empty parking lot next to a service station.

Linda rolled down the window to shout for help, and the station attendant called an ambulance. Linda's grandfather had suffered a heart attack, but he did not die. For the rest of his life, he told the story of how his ten-year-old granddaughter had steered the car through traffic to safety. But Linda always corrected him, saying that an angel had come to the rescue.

Angel in the Snow

Another child who was saved by an angel was nine-year-old Buddy. Buddy had recently been made an **altar boy**. The first mass at which he would serve was to be held at six o'clock in the morning. When Buddy awoke on the big day, however, he found that a heavy snow had fallen during the night and snow-plows had not yet cleared the streets. Since Buddy

A young boy walks through the snow. An angel is said to have saved a boy from freezing in the snow.

did not live too far from the church, his mother reluctantly agreed to let him walk.

The walk was much harder than Buddy had expected. The snow was 2 feet deep (.6m). By the time he got to the church, he was cold and very tired. He was also disappointed to find that no one else was there. He was the only one who had braved the snow to come to the church that morning.

After resting for a while, Buddy started to make his way home again. The wind was against him now, and he was becoming exhausted. Just when he felt he could not go on, a man came up behind him. He had a scarf covering most of his face, but his eyes were friendly, and Buddy was not afraid. The man picked Buddy up, put him on his shoulders, and began to walk.

The man carried Buddy all the way to his front doorstep, even though Buddy had not told him where he lived. After the man had gently helped him down, Buddy turned to thank him, only to find that he was gone. And although there were footprints leading up to the door, there were no footprints leading away. Buddy never saw the man again, but he says, "I know he is still here, ready to help me again when I need him."[13]

Saved from Drowning

Jean Hannan Ondracek was also saved by a mysterious stranger. On vacation at a resort one summer, she decided to go swimming by herself while her friends stayed on the shore to sunbathe. No lifeguards were on duty, and Ondracek was alone in the lake. She swam for quite a while, going farther out into the lake than she meant to. Suddenly, she felt short of breath and very tired. The water was deep, and Ondracek knew that she did not have the energy to make it back to shore. She tried calling to her friends, but she was too far out to be heard.

Aware that she could drown, Ondracek prayed for help. It was at that moment that she saw an old canoe off to her left. She swam to the canoe, but she was disappointed to find that it was in very bad shape and was anchored to the bottom of the lake. She could not use it to paddle to the shore. Ondracek held onto the boat and tried to catch her breath. She was afraid to let go and try to swim to shore, but she also knew she could not hold on to the decaying boat for long.

Clear, blue water entices a swimmer. One swimmer, who became short of breath, says an angel helped her reach the shore safely.

Ondracek was crying in despair when a man swam up to her and asked if she needed help. She had not seen the man approach and did not know where he had come from. The man said that he was a safety inspector. He encouraged her to swim the distance back to shore and promised her help if she needed it, saying, "I'll swim beside you the whole way, until you reach shore. If you get in any trouble, I'll hold you up."[14]

An illustration from a nineteenth-century book shows a youngster in an angel's arms.

With the safety inspector's encouragement, Ondracek found the strength to swim back to shore. He swam close beside her the entire time. When she finally stumbled onto the shore, her friends asked her why she had been gone so long. Ondracek told them that she would have drowned if it had not been for the lifeguard who swam beside her the entire way. Her friends were puzzled because there was no one in the water, and no one anywhere near them on the beach. Ondracek's mysterious safety inspector had disappeared. When she later found out that there were no lifeguards or safety inspectors at the resort, she was convinced that she had been saved by an angel.

T.J.'s Angel

Although many people report angels saving them from accidental death, other people have angel encounters that result in a miraculous healing. Robin Nisius and her four-year-old son, T.J., had just such an encounter. T.J. had been battling **leukemia** and had fallen into a **coma**. The doctors did not expect him to wake up and told his mother that he would probably die during the night. Nisius prayed for strength while she sat by T.J.'s bed. Suddenly T.J. sat up. He cried to his mother and told her he was frightened. He said, "The angels are here, Mommy, and they want me to go with them now." [15]

Nisius fell to her knees and began praying for her son's life, begging God not to take him at such a young age. T.J. gazed around the room as if he could see something that his mother could not. Then he smiled and closed his eyes. Nisius, sure that her son had died, gathered him in her arms. She was relieved to find however, that he was still alive. Nisius rocked T.J. as she continued to cry and pray.

After a few minutes Nisius felt a gentle presence. Although she could not see anyone, she was sure that someone was nearby. Nisuis describes what happened next:

> My heart seemed to lighten and a sense of calm came over me that I had never before experienced. Then, as I looked at his sweet face in the darkness, I saw a hand tenderly stroke his cheek as he lay in my arms. As soon as I saw it, it was gone, but whatever or whoever it was left behind a wonderful feeling of peace.[16]

T.J. woke from the coma the next morning.

The Power of Prayer

Studies have shown that a positive attitude can speed the healing process. People who pray are usually confident that their prayers will be answered. It is possible that people are healed not by angels, but rather by their own positive prayers and thoughts.

In this fifteenth-century painting, the artist coveys an angel's sense of calm and strength, traits that all people find appealing.

Whether an angel encounter results in a dramatic healing, as in T.J.'s case, or simply in a feeling of peace and well-being, most people who have had one say that the experience changed their lives in some way. For some people the change was a small one; the feeling that they were being watched over brought them a lifelong sense of calm. For others the change was more dramatic, resulting in a new outlook on life or a decision to do something differently than they had planned. People who have had angel encounters are sure that angels are real, and they take comfort in this knowledge.

Notes

Chapter 2: Angels That Bring Comfort

1. Quoted in Sophy Burnham, *A Book of Angels*. New York: Ballantine, 1990, p. 318.
2. Quoted in Dorren Virture, *Angel Visions*. Carlsbad, CA: Hay House, 2000, p. 14.
3. Quoted in Virture, *Angel Visions*, p. 15.
4. Quoted in Joan Wester Anderson, *Where Angels Walk*. Sea Cliff, NY: Barton & Brett, 1992, p. 117.
5. Quoted in Nancy Gibbs, "Angels Among Us," *Time*, December 29, 1993.
6. Quoted in Gibbs, "Angels Among Us," *Time*.

Chapter 3: Angels with a Message

7. Quoted in Glennyce S. Eckersley, *Teen Angel*. London: Rider, 2003, p. 129.
8. Quoted in Joan Wester Anderson, *An Angel to Watch over Me*. New York: Ballantine, 1994, p. 41.
9. Quoted in Eckersley, *Teen Angel*, p. 80.
10. Quoted in Marilynn Webber, *A Rustle of Angels*. Riverside, CA: Zondervan, 1994. Available online at www.beliefnet.com/story/16/story_1656_1.html.

11. Quoted in Charles Lindbergh, *The Spirit of St. Louis*. New York: Charles Scribner's Sons, 1953, p. 389.

Chapter 4: Saved by an Angel

12. Quoted in Brad Steiger and Sherry Hansen Steiger, *Angels over Their Shoulders*. New York: Fawcett Columbine, 1995, p. 38.
13. Quoted in Anderson, *An Angel to Watch over Me*, p. 47.
14. Quoted in Anderson, *Where Angels Walk*, p. 43.
15. Quoted in Jamie C. Miller, Laura Lewis, and Jennifer Basye Sander, *Heavenly Miracles*. New York: HarperCollins, 2000, p. 44.
16. Quoted in Miller, Lewis, and Sander, *Heavenly Miracles*, p. 45.

Glossary

altar boy: A boy who assists the priest during a religious service.

coma: A state of prolonged deep unconsciousness.

deception: The act of intentionally making someone believe what is not true.

demonic possession: When an evil spirit enters a person's body and uses it for its own purposes.

guardian angel: An angel believed to watch over and protect one particular person.

halo: A ring of light that surrounds the head of an angel or saint.

leukemia: A usually fatal form of cancer in which the body produces too many white blood cells.

mourning: A time of deep sadness for someone who has died.

tumor: An abnormal mass of tissue that has no useful function. A tumor can be a sign of cancer.

For Further Exploration

Books

Joan Wester Anderson, *An Angel to Watch over Me.* New York: Ballantine, 1994. In this book readers will find accounts of children's encounters with angels. The book also includes a section with angel songs, poems, and prayers for children. There is also an angel quiz.

Joanna Crosse, *A Child's Book of Angels.* Cambridge, MA: Barefoot, 2000. Told in a storybook format, this beautifully illustrated book is full of information about angels.

Mimi Doe, *Drawing Angels Near.* New York: Atria, 1997. This is a book of angel encounters told and illustrated by children.

Clair Llewellyn, *Saints and Angels.* New York: Kingfisher, 2003. This beautifully illustrated book includes a section on angels. Choirs of angels, guardian angels, and fallen angels are covered.

Metropolitan Museum of Art, *I Imagine Angels.* New York: Atheneum, 2000. This is a book of angel-themed poems and prayers for children, enhanced with artwork from the Metropolitan Museum of Art.

Marty Noble, *Color Your Own Angels in Art Master-pieces*. Mineola, NY: Dover, 2003. In this book children can color angel paintings by famous artists, including Botticelli and Raphael.

Web Sites

Angel Realm (www.angelrealm.com/menu.htm). This site features descriptions of many angel encounters.

Angels Online (www.angels-online.com/index.html). This site is devoted to angels and includes many stories of angel encounters. Users may also send in stories of their own angel encounters.

Encounters with Angels: An Interview with Emma Heathcote (http://accessnewage.com/articles/vario/GFANGELS.HTM). This interview details the work of Emma Heathcote, who investigates angel encounters. It includes statistics about the kinds of encounters people have.

Index